Manuel de F
arranged by
Ernesto Halffter
[1942]

DANZA RITUAL DEL FUEGO

from
El amor brujo

cello and orchestra

Score
with cello part inserted

WARNING: the photocopying of any pages of this publication is illegal. If copies are made in breach of copyright, the Publishers will, where possible, sue for damages.

Every illegal copy means a lost sale. Lost sales lead to shorter print runs and rising prices. Soon the music goes out of print, and more fine works are lost from the repertoire.

CH 61115

CHESTER MUSIC

(A division of Music Sales Ltd.)
8/9 Frith Street LONDON W1V 5TZ
tel. 0171 434 0066 fax 0171 287 6329
Exclusive distributors: Music Sales Ltd.
Newmarket Road, Bury St Edmunds, Suffolk IP33 3YB
tel. 01284 702600 fax 01284 702592
Web: http://www.musicsales.co.uk   e-mail: music@musicsales.co.uk

The *Ritual Fire Dance* from *El amor brujo*, arranged for cello and orchestra by Ernesto Halffter, was first performed on 20 December 1942 by Guilhermina Suggia, cello, with the National Symphony Orchestra conducted by Pedro de Freitas Branco.

La *Danza Ritual del Fuego* de *El amor brujo*, arreglado para violonchelo y orquesta por Ernesto Halffter, fue representado por primera vez el 20 de diciembre 1942 por Guilhermina Suggia, violonchelo, con la Orquesta Sinfónica Nacional dirigida por Pedro de Freitas Branco.

La *Danse Rituelle de Feu*, tirée d'*El amor brujo* et adaptée pour violoncelle et orchestre par Ernesto Halffter, fut jouée pour la première fois le 20 décembre 1942 par Guilhermina Suggia, violoncelliste, avec l'Orchestre National Symphonique dirigé par Pedro de Freitas Branco.

ORCHESTRATION

Solo cello

2 Flutes (one doubling piccolo)
Oboe
2 Clarinets in B flat
Bassoon
2 Horns in F
Timpani
Piano
Strings

NOTE

This arrangement of the *Danza ritual del Fuego* from *El Amor Brujo* was made for performance at a gala concert in Lisbon to celebrate the official visit to Portugal by the Spanish Minister for Foreign Affairs in 1942.

The concert featured Portuguese cellist Guilhermina Suggia, who was to play a piece for cello and orchestra. However, as the only available version for solo cello was with piano accompaniment (by Gregor Piatigorsky [CH 00933]), my father, then living in Lisbon, was asked to make this arrangement.

Manuel Halffter

NOTA

Esta adaptación de la *Danza Ritual del Fuego* de *El amor brujo* fue creado para representar en un concierto de gala en Lisboa para celebrar la visita oficial a Portugal del Ministerio de Asuntos Exteriores Español en 1942.

El concierto presentó a la violonchelista Portuguesa Guilhermina Suggia, que debía tocar una pieza para violonchelo y orquesta. Como la única versión disponible para violonchelo solo fue con acompañamiento para piano, (de Gregor Piatigorsky [CH 00933]), pidieron a mi padre, que vivía entonces en Lisboa, que hiciera esta adaptación.

Manuel Halffter

NOTE

Cette adaptation de la *Danza Ritual del Fuego* tirée d'*El amor brujo* fut créée en 1942 pour la représentation d'un concert de gala donnée a Lisbonne en l'honneur de la visite officielle au Portugal du Ministre espagnol des Affaires Etrangères.

Pour ce concert, la violoncelliste portugaise Guilhermina Suggia devait jouer un morceau pour violoncelle et orchestre. Comme il n'existait qu'une version pour violoncelle avec accompagnement au piano (par Gregor Piatigorsky [CH 00933]), on demanda à mon père, vivant alors à Lisbonne, de faire cet arrangement.

Manuel Halffter

DANZA RITUAL DEL FUEGO

(Para ahuyentar los malos espíritus)

MANUEL DE FALLA
arr. Ernesto Halffter

© Copyright 1996 Chester Music Limited

All Rights Reserved

12

16

18